D0102045

30130503365589

MINEOLA FIRE
MINEOLA F.D.

TRUCKS

James Nixon

W
FRANKLIN WATTS
LONDON•SYDNEY

 An Appleseed Editions book

First published in 2010 by Franklin Watts
338 Euston Road, London NW1 3BH

Franklin Watts Australia
Hachette Children's Books
Level 17/207 Kent St, Sydney, NSW 2000

Created by Appleseed Editions Ltd,
Well House, Friars Hill, Guestling,
East Sussex TN35 4ET

Planning and production by Discovery Books Limited
Designed by D.R. ink
Cover design by Blink Media
Edited by James Nixon

ISBN: 978 1 4451 0033 3

Dewey Classification: 629.2'24

A CIP catalogue for this book is available from the British Library.

Photograph acknowledgements
Alamy Images: pp. 13 bottom (Paul Collis), 15 bottom (MiRafoto.com), 16 bottom (Gaspar R. Avila), 22 (Imagebroker), 23 (Imagebroker), 29 bottom (Stuart Walker); Getty Images: pp. 4 top (Dorling Kindersley), 9 top (Justin Sullivan), 12 (E. Neitzel), 25 top (Tariq Mahmood/AFP); Istockphoto.com; pp. 21 top (Barbara Sauder), 28 (Elton Dralle), 29 top; Photolibrary: p. 17 (Javier Larrea); Renault Trucks: p. 10; Shutterstock: pp. 4 bottom (Tyler Olson), 5 bottom (James Steidl), 6 (Max Blain), 7 top (Jack Cronkhite), 7 bottom (Javier Sanchez), 8 (Jo Lin), 9 bottom, 13 top (Dale A. Stork), 14 (Slavko Sereda), 15 top (Vibrant Image Studio), 16 top, 18 top (Jim Lopes), 18 bottom (Monkey Business Images), 19 (DESmith Photography), 20 top (Daniel Goodchild), 20 bottom (Cary Kalscheuer), 21 bottom, 25 bottom (Zavodskov Anatoliy Nikolaevich), 26 (Ivaschenko Roman); Side Dump Industries: p. 27 (Pete Laskie/JD Gordon Advertising); Volvo Trucks: pp. 5 top, 11; Wikimedia: p. 24.

Cover photos: Shutterstock: top (Mikael Damkier), bottom (Fernando Rodrigues).

Printed in China

Franklin Watts is a division of Hachette Children's Books,
www.hachette.co.uk

Contents

What is a truck?

Trucks are large, powerful machines which carry huge loads. They can haul anything from heavy logs or milk to large cranes or racing cars.

A truck is made of two sections. The cab is where the driver sits. Behind it is the trailer where the load is carried.

Chassis: Trucks need a strong body. The chassis is the main steel frame.

Engine: To move a big truck you need a powerful engine. The driver can check the engine by tilting the cab forward.

18-wheelers

The biggest trucks on the road have eighteen wheels! Each axle on the trailer holds four wheels.

Axles: For extra support large trucks have extra wheels. They are attached to the ends of axles.

Exhaust: Fumes from the engine are carried away by the exhaust pipes.

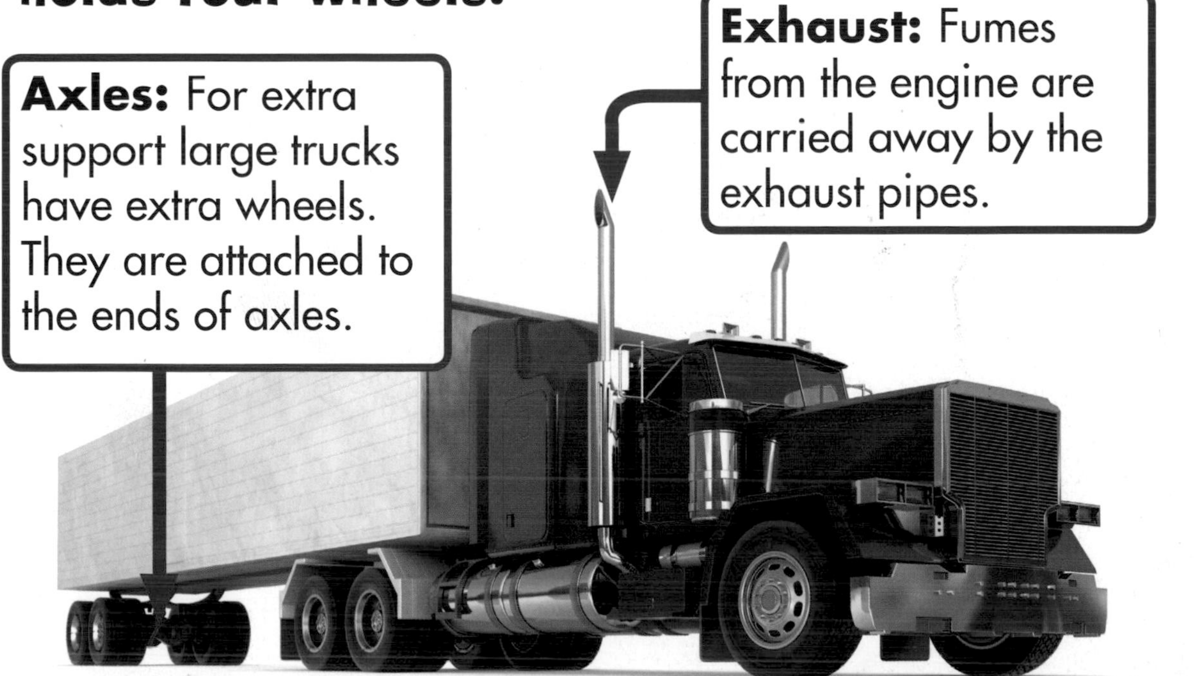

Articulated trucks

Some trucks come all in one piece, but on big articulated trucks the trailer and cab are separate. They link together with a special coupling device.

The trailer cannot move by itself because it has wheels at the rear end only.

This articulated truck is carrying a huge storage unit called a **container**. The container is lifted on and off with a crane.

Coupling device

The trailer slots into a horseshoe-shaped metal plate behind the cab (right). This link lets the truck bend when it goes around corners. A trailer can be quickly unhooked and replaced with another one.

Road trains

Sometimes trucks can pull more than one trailer. In Australia, trucks tow three or four trailers, sometimes more! These are called road trains. Imagine trying to overtake one of these!

Tankers

Tankers are trucks with long, tube-shaped trailers. They carry liquid loads, such as petrol or milk. A tanker keeps the milk cool, just like a fridge does.

Tanks are split into compartments to stop the liquid sloshing around too much. Each compartment is unloaded using hoses and **valves** on the side of the truck.

Concrete mixers

Concrete mixers carry concrete in huge drums to building sites. During the journey the drum spins around to mix the concrete.

In the cab

The driver's controls in a truck are like the ones you would find in a car. There is a steering wheel, gear changer and indicators. There are lots of display panels to tell the driver how the truck is working.

The windscreens on trucks are large so the driver can see everything clearly.

Dashboard

Panels on the dashboard show the driver the speed, the amount of fuel left in the tank, and how many miles or kilometres he or she has travelled.

Mobile home

Truck drivers may spend days on the road. This means the cab must also make a comfy home. At the back of the cab, the driver has a bed, fridge, TV and a cooking area.

Tow trucks

When a car breaks down or has an accident, tow trucks come to the rescue.

A hook lifts the vehicle on to the back of the tow truck. It is then fastened and towed away to the garage to be fixed.

Winch

Some tow trucks have a **winch** to pull out vehicles that have crashed off the road into a field or ditch.

Winch

The winch winds a cable in to pull the vehicle up. The cable is made out of very strong metal wires.

Heavy tow trucks

Heavy-duty tow trucks can recover even the largest vehicles. They could pull an 18-wheeler if they needed too!

Car transporters

Car transporters are trucks specially designed to carry new cars to the showroom.

Each car sits on a ramp called a deck. They are strapped down tightly so they don't roll off.

Decks

The cars are driven on to the decks carefully. The ramps are then raised up more so more cars can fit on underneath. The vehicles are tilted at an angle to make more room. Some transporters hold up to 12 cars.

Moving racecars

Motor racing teams carry their racecars and equipment inside the trailer of a truck. The outside of the truck is painted with the team name and colours.

Mobile cranes

A mobile crane is a truck with a crane on its back. The crane can be easily moved between worksites. Some truck cranes can carry a load as they travel!

Big lifters

The biggest truck cranes can lift up to 1200 tonnes. That is the same as 1200 cars. The huge arm of some cranes can extend to over 100 m. This is the length of a football pitch!

Outriggers

Before the crane lifts anything the outriggers must be set up. These are four legs that keep the truck steady when it lifts heavy objects.

The crane is fitted to a turntable on the truck, so that it can turn.

Cab

On the turntable is a cab where the crane is operated. The operator pulls and pushes levers to turn the crane around and move it up and down.

Fire trucks

Fire engines are fast trucks. They rush to an emergency with sirens blaring. All the firefighters' equipment is on board.

Tools such as lights, masks and cutting equipment are kept behind shutters. Ladders lie on the roof.

Water is pumped on to a fire from a huge water tank inside the truck.

Turntable ladder

Some fire trucks have an extra-long ladder for reaching the tops of tall buildings. This is attached to a turntable on top of the truck.

The ladder is also **telescopic**, which means it can be made longer. Some have a platform at the top and a hose with a water supply running through the whole ladder.

Rubbish trucks

What happens to all the rubbish you throw away at home? It is probably collected and taken away in a truck.

On some rubbish trucks your wheelie bin's contents are lifted and tipped in automatically (left). Inside the truck, the rubbish is crushed and packed up tight.

Grapple trucks

If we throw away large items, such as pieces of furniture, a different type of truck is needed. This grapple truck has a long arm that can grab and lift a heavy load.

After the rubbish has been collected from your house another truck may take it to a landfill site. This is a huge hole in the ground where rubbish is dumped. The truck tips the waste out.

Racing trucks

Trucks are huge, bulky vehicles. Yet they can be raced around race tracks just like cars. Truck racing is a fast and exciting sport.

Only the front part of a truck is raced. Parts of racing trucks have been changed to make them faster and safer.

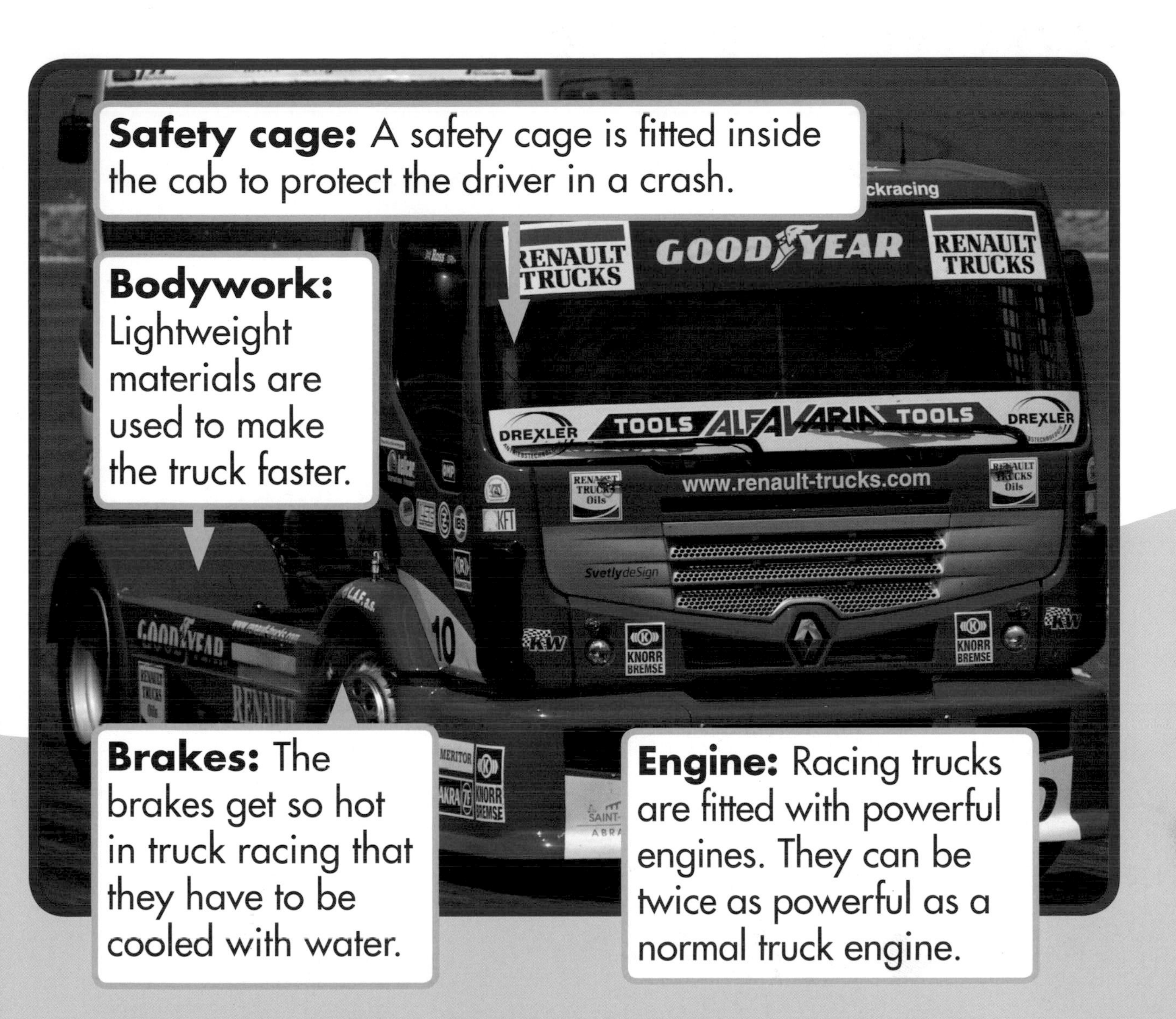

Truck racing facts

- **Racing trucks are limited to 100 mph (160 kph). Above that speed would be unsafe.**
- **Driving a truck without its trailer is called bobtailing.**

Off-road trucks

Not all trucks are designed for the road. Off-road trucks can tackle rough and bumpy ground.

Chassis

The **chassis** on an off-roader is high off the ground so that the truck does not get stuck on rocks.

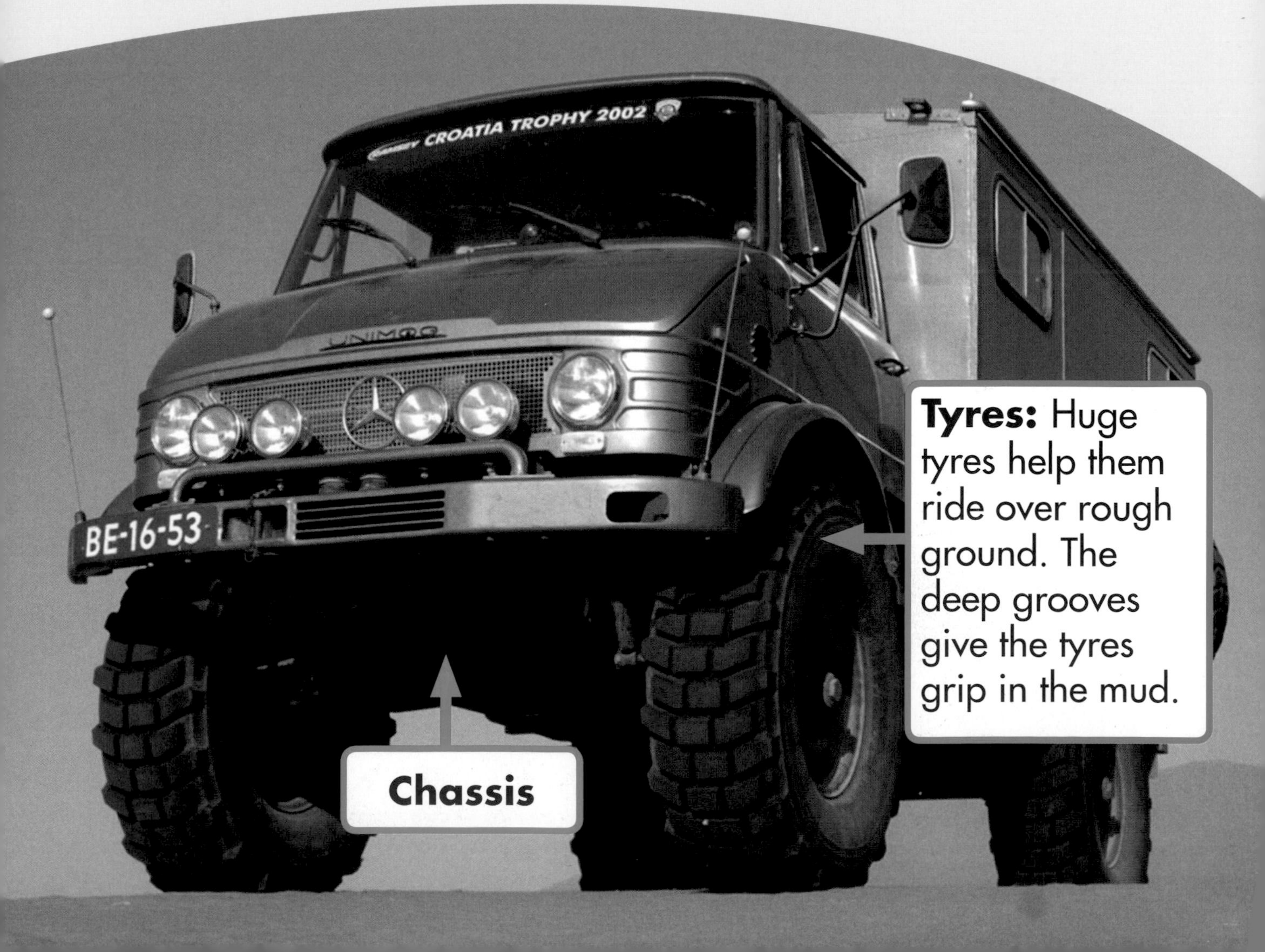

Tyres: Huge tyres help them ride over rough ground. The deep grooves give the tyres grip in the mud.

Chassis

Off-road trucks have many uses. The army use them to transport troops and heavy equipment. Loggers need off-road trucks to carry timber through the forest.

Dump trucks

Dump trucks are used to carry building materials, such as sand, earth and rocks. These trucks can carry loads twice their own weight.

Tipper

To dump its load, the truck's back is lifted up using **hydraulic rams**. A liquid is pushed into the tubes of the ram forcing the tipper up. The load then slides out.

Side dumping

Usually loads are dropped off the back of a dump truck. But some dump trucks are different. This tipper's hydraulic rams tilt the tipper on its side. Other dump trucks drop their loads out of the bottom of the trailer.

Giant trucks

Some trucks carry enormous loads. The biggest dump trucks do not drive on roads. They work at **quarries** and **mines**. They take away the rocks that have been dug up by diggers.

Mighty machine

The Liebherr T282B is the largest mining truck. It is big enough to carry a load of nearly 400 tonnes. The cab is so high that the driver needs a ladder to reach it!

Wide loads

There are huge trucks on the road, too. They carry loads that are so big that the police must drive in front to warn other drivers. On a **low-loader** (below) the truck's trailer is low to the ground. This is so large loads can be loaded and unloaded easily.

This low-loader is carrying a massive mining truck.

Glossary

articulated truck a truck that is split into two sections

axle a bar with wheels attached

bobtailing driving a truck without its trailer

chassis the frame to which parts of a vehicle are attached

coupling device a device which connects a trailer to the cab of a truck

container a large metal box that fits on a truck's trailer. It is used for transporting lots of smaller items.

grapple truck a truck that picks up and loads bulky waste with a grappling arm

hydraulic power which results from pushing liquid through a tube

low-loader a lorry with a low trailer with no sides, for transporting heavy loads

mine a place where coal or other rocks or minerals are dug out from underground

quarry a place where stone is removed from the ground by digging

ram the rod which powers the tipper on a dump truck

telescopic having parts that slide into one another. A telescopic ladder can be extended and shortened again.

valve a device for controlling the movement of fluid through a pipe

winch a machine which lifts up heavy objects with a strong cable

Index

Websites

www.sparky.org/firetruck/index.htm
Find out more about fire trucks.

www.britishtruckracing.co.uk
Official site of the British Truck Racing Association, with news of upcoming races.

www.uk-trucking.net/juniortruckers/index.asp
This site explains how trucks work, the history of trucks and the different types of truck.